KU-502-438

CONTENTS

CHUCK YEAGER

FASTER THAN SOUND

On 14 October 1947, American test pilot Chuck Yeager eased himself into the cockpit of the Bell X-1. At the controls of this rocket-powered plane, Yeager was attempting to become the very first person to fly supersonic – faster than the speed of sound. He was risking his life in the process, so the stakes could not have been higher.

Going supersonic

In the late 1940s, the United States, United Kingdom, Germany, France, and the Soviet Union were all competing to be the first to fly at supersonic speed, known as Mach 1. So far everyone had failed. When approaching Mach 1, pilots had experienced severe shaking as pressure waves buffeted their planes. Flight controls had frozen or malfunctioned. Several planes had crashed or broken up in mid-air.

Yeager's Bell X-1 was named *Glamorous Glennis* after his wife. The plane was painted bright orange to make it visible as it sped through the sky.

Keeping control

Even though the Bell X-1 was fitted with special flight controls to maintain command at supersonic speed, many people believed that it was simply impossible to fly that fast. Furthermore, things were not looking good for the test flight. Yeager had broken two ribs in a horse-riding accident shortly before. He had not told his seniors for fear that they would not let him fly. Now, as he climbed into the cockpit, every move was agony.

TOOLS OF THE TRADE

The Bell X-1 had few safety features. In particular, there was no ejector seat, so the pilot could not exit the plane in an emergency. The plane's fuel, a mixture of alcohol and liquid oxygen, was kept at −182 degrees Celsius (−297 degrees Fahrenheit) and stored under the pilot's seat. This made the plane colder than a freezer!

Yeager made his own headgear from a leather football helmet. He cut out holes for earphones and an oxygen supply!

Launching the Bell X-1

In order to conserve the Bell X-1's fuel, a B-29 bomber carried the plane to the test altitude. As the bomber neared the correct height, Yeager climbed into his cockpit and gave the thumbs-up. The B-29 dropped the plane like a gliding missile. Yeager burst from the darkness into dazzling light. After diving to gain speed, he pointed the Bell X-1's nose upwards and fired all four rocket engines. The thrust slammed him back in his seat. What a ride!

"[The flight] was smooth as a baby's bottom. Grandma could be sitting up there sipping lemonade."
Chuck Yeager

The Bell X-1 loading into the bomb bay of the B-29 bomber, *Superfortress*, which carried Yeager to test height.

UNITED STATES AIR FORCE

Mach 1 at last

Yeager had made eight previous attempts to reach Mach 1 without success. This time, as he approached supersonic speed, he felt the familiar shaking, like racing a car along a rocky road. However, as he flew faster, something unexpected happened – the ride became smoother. Yeager watched the speedometer needle drop off the scale. He was flying supersonic! A deafening boom echoed across the desert below as his plane broke through the sound barrier. Yeager's fuel lasted just 2½ minutes. After achieving Mach 1, Yeager cut the engines and glided down to a safe landing.

A plane makes a "sonic boom" as it accelerates through the pressure waves caused by its own passage and breaks the sound barrier. To people watching, it looks as though the plane is passing through a disc-shaped cloud in the sky.

Faster and faster

Yeager's flight marked the dawn of the jet age, when test planes flew faster and faster. In 1953, a plane flew at Mach 2, twice the speed of sound. In 1967, an X-15 test plane flew at Mach 6.7. At around 7,300 kilometres per hour (4,535 miles per hour), this is twice the speed that a rifle bullet travels through the air. The supersonic airliner *Concorde* flew at Mach 2 as it ferried passengers between London and New York from 1976 to 2003. In 2004, an X-43 scramjet reached Mach 9.6.

50 USA

Jacqueline
Cochran
Pioneer Pilot

1996

In the mid-1990s, this stamp was issued to celebrate America's pioneering and daring female test pilot Jacqueline Cochran, who is thought to have set more than 200 flying records in her lifetime.

Supersonic women

In the 1950s and 1960s, two female pilots, Jacqueline Auriol from France and American aviator Jacqueline Cochran, competed to be the "fastest woman in the world". Both women flew at supersonic speed in 1953 and had reached Mach 2 by 1960. In 1963, Auriol achieved her top speed of 2,039 kilometres per hour (1,274 miles per hour). But Cochran flew even faster in 1964, becoming the overall winner.

Adventures in the sky

Yeager's achievement opened up amazing opportunities for adventures in flight. However, modern flying is not only about going faster. In June 1979, an extraordinary flying machine flew a slow and wobbly course across the English Channel, a distance of 35 kilometres (22 miles). Why was it amazing? Expert hang-glider and cyclist Bryan Allen was making the first human-powered flight across the Channel in a pedal-driven plane.

Allen's feat marked the start of a new age in which men and women would extend the limits of flying not just in planes, but also in balloons, spacecraft, and even rocket-powered jetpacks. This book charts some of their most daring feats. So strap on your crash helmet for a roller-coaster ride through the thrills, spills, and triumphs of modern aviation!

Bryan Allen pedalled across the English Channel in 1979 in a precarious-looking bicycle with wings. Two years earlier he had achieved the first-ever human-powered flight.

RUTAN AND YEAGER
NEVER TOUCH DOWN

On 14 December 1986, former fighter pilot Dick Rutan and his partner Jeana Yeager prepared for takeoff in a unique, ultralight plane. Their aim was to complete the first-ever non-stop flight around the world without refuelling. Aeronautical engineer Burt Rutan, Dick's younger brother, had designed their plane, which was called *Voyager*. However, there were serious doubts as to whether *Voyager* would even get off the ground.

Heavy with fuel

Previous round-the-world flights had stopped many times to refuel. Rutan and Yeager (no relation to Chuck Yeager – see page 4) were aiming to fly the whole way non-stop. To meet this challenge, *Voyager* had to carry all the fuel it would need for the journey. This made the plane extremely heavy and dangerously unstable. In fact, before the start of the trip, it had never taken off with full tanks!

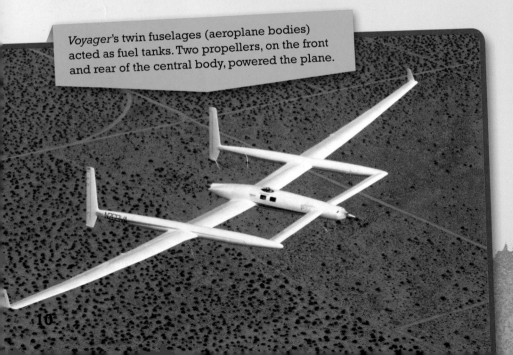

Voyager's twin fuselages (aeroplane bodies) acted as fuel tanks. Two propellers, on the front and rear of the central body, powered the plane.

When the moment arrived for final takeoff, Rutan urged the plane along the world's longest runway at Edwards Air Force Base, California. *Voyager*'s wing tips screeched along the ground. With only 243 metres (800 feet) of runway left, the plane finally became airborne, wings buckling under the strain. The challenge was on!

Global Missions

US Army Air Service crews flying two biplanes made the first round-the-world flight in 1924. They stopped 72 times to refuel and took 175 days to complete the trip. In 1933, solo American pilot Wiley Post completed 25,000 kilometres (15,500 miles) around the world in under 8 days. He also touched down to refuel. In 1949, the Boeing B-50 *Lucky Lady II* flew around the world non-stop in 93 hours, but refuelled four times in the air.

Jeana Yeager standing in the cockpit of *Voyager* talking to Dick Rutan. Conditions were very cramped on board *Voyager*. The cockpit was just 60 centimetres (2 feet) wide.

11

Go west

After takeoff, *Voyager* headed west over the vast Pacific Ocean. Rutan and Yeager were on their own at last! To conserve fuel, they flew much lower than a passenger aircraft, but they also had to waste fuel dodging thunderstorms – and a hurricane, Typhoon Marge, which could have wrecked their fragile craft. On Day Five, they had to climb to 6,000 metres (20,000 feet) to avoid towering thunderclouds over Africa, and both pilots suffered from lack of oxygen. They flew onwards, averaging just 175 kilometres per hour (110 miles per hour), which is much slower than a jet aircraft. Flying any faster would also have wasted fuel. The journey was stressful and exhausting for both pilots.

A near disaster

During the night of Day Eight, and almost with the end of their voyage in sight, disaster threatened – a fuel pump failed. For a nerve-wracking 5 minutes, *Voyager* glided without power before the engines restarted. Then, 9 days and 3 minutes after setting out, *Voyager* touched down back at Edwards Air Force Base, earning Rutan and Yeager a place in the record books.

1 Takeoff at Edwards Air Force Base, California

2 Rutan and Yeager have to dodge Typhoon Marge

3 Thunderclouds over Africa force them to climb

4 On Day Seven, Rutan suffers from extreme exhaustion

5 Fuel-pump failure – engine stalls for 5 minutes

6 Safe landing back at Edwards Air Force Base

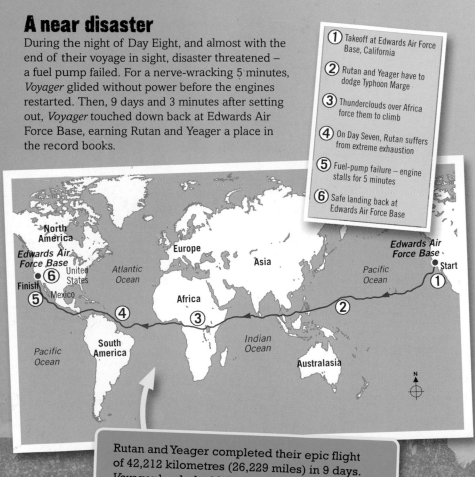

Rutan and Yeager completed their epic flight of 42,212 kilometres (26,229 miles) in 9 days. *Voyager* landed with less than two per cent of its fuel left in its tanks.

Steve Fossett

In 2005, 19 years after Rutan and Yeager's record-breaking flight, the American millionaire businessman and aviator Steve Fossett achieved the first solo non-stop round-the-world flight without refuelling. Like *Voyager*, Fossett's plane *GlobalFlyer* was designed by Burt Rutan. Fossett achieved his own epic journey in just 67 hours – less than 3 days.

Steve Fossett smiling from inside the tiny cockpit of his round-the-world aircraft, *GlobalFlyer*.

PICCARD AND JONES AROUND THE WORLD

On 1 March 1999, inhabitants of the small village of Château-d'Oex in Switzerland watched as a tall, silver-coloured balloon rose into the sky and floated away. The tiny gondola (cabin) beneath it carried Swiss aviator Bertrand Piccard and British balloonist Brian Jones. The balloon was called *Breitling Orbiter 3* and its mission was to fly around the world.

Unpredictable flight

Hot-air balloons rise when the air inside them is heated, so that it becomes lighter than the cold air outside. The balloon is then carried along by the wind. Manned balloon flights began in the 1780s. For the following two centuries, people flew balloons for sport, research, and exploration. But balloon flight was too unpredictable to travel long distances.

Then and now

In September 1783, the Montgolfier brothers of France launched a hot-air balloon carrying a sheep, a duck, and a cockerel – the first time a hot-air balloon had carried living things. Later in 1783, two French noblemen made the first hot-air balloon flight to carry people.

The King of France watched as the Mongolfiers' balloon rose into the air in 1783. The flight lasted 8 minutes and the balloon travelled 3 kilometres (2 miles).

Better understanding

By the late 1970s, improved technology and an understanding of weather systems led to a new age in long-distance ballooning. In 1978, three Americans crossed the Atlantic Ocean in a balloon. In 1995, millionaire aviator Steve Fossett (see page 13) ballooned across the Pacific Ocean. Only one great ballooning challenge remained – to circumnavigate (or circle) the globe, without touching down.

The *Breitling Orbiter 3* soars over the Swiss Alps in March 1999. Bertrand Piccard and Brian Jones are inside the red gondola hanging below.

The sport of millionaires

In the 1990s, the race to be first to fly around the world in a balloon became a contest between two millionaires, Steve Fossett and British businessman Richard Branson. After several failed attempts each, Fossett and Branson teamed up in 1998 to try again. Their balloon, the *ICO Global Challenger*, used the latest technology, but came down in the Pacific Ocean before completing its challenge. Piccard and Jones could now make their own attempt to set the record.

Using the jet stream

After taking to the air on 1 March 1999, *Breitling Orbiter 3* headed southwards from Switzerland. It crossed the Mediterranean to Northwest Africa, where Piccard and Jones hoped to pick up powerful winds, known as the jet stream, that blow at high altitudes. Understanding the jet stream was instrumental in enabling balloonists to fly long distances.

The Piccard Family

Bertrand Piccard came from a long line of scientists and adventurers. His grandfather Auguste Piccard invented the pressurized gondola in 1930. This allowed balloonists to ascend to heights that would previously have killed them through lack of oxygen. He also invented machines to explore underwater. Bertrand's father Jacques Piccard was an underwater explorer. In 1960, he and Don Walsh of the US Navy were the first to descend to the ocean's deepest point in the Pacific, in a submarine.

In 1931, Auguste Piccard (wearing the hat) reached a height of 15,781 metres (51,775 feet) in a balloon. He is pictured here a year later, standing next to the pressurized cabin that he invented.

The *ICO Global Challenger* came
down in the Pacific Ocean after
only 7 days in flight. Fossett,
Branson, and a third pilot,
Per Lindstrand, had to leap
into the water to be rescued.

This entire metal structure was attached to the *Breitling Orbiter 3* balloon. It includes the gondola in which Piccard and Jones lived during their journey, and the oxygen tanks that enabled them to breathe. The small cabin contained navigation and communications equipment, a pressure toilet, and bunk beds.

Heading east

Picking up the jet stream above North Africa, *Breitling Orbiter 3* headed almost due east. Crossing Africa, India, and China, the crew reached the Pacific Ocean on Day Eleven. Every day, Piccard and Jones took one 8-hour shift at the controls each, and spent 8 hours resting in their bunks. They spent the remaining 8 hours of the day on joint tasks.

The balloon drifted at an average height of 9,100 metres (30,000 feet). Tanks on the outside of the gondola piped in the oxygen the pair needed to stay alive. The gondola was heated, but the air temperature was so cold that sometimes the temperature inside the cabin dropped below freezing. Ice regularly had to be cleared from the instruments.

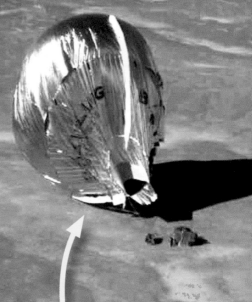

Breitling Orbiter 3 lands in the Egyptian desert to complete an amazing adventure that set six world records!

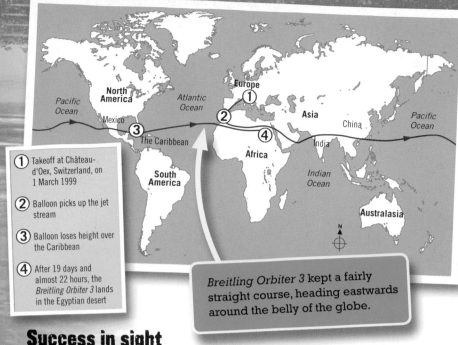

① Takeoff at Château-d'Oex, Switzerland, on 1 March 1999

② Balloon picks up the jet stream

③ Balloon loses height over the Caribbean

④ After 19 days and almost 22 hours, the *Breitling Orbiter 3* lands in the Egyptian desert

Breitling Orbiter 3 kept a fairly straight course, heading eastwards around the belly of the globe.

Success in sight

After crossing the Pacific Ocean, the balloonists passed over Mexico. As they approached the Caribbean, the balloon rapidly lost height. Piccard and Jones had to burn much of their fuel to regain that height and pick up favourable winds. After that, crossing the Atlantic Ocean went smoothly. The balloon completed its round trip over Northwest Africa, continuing east to land in the Egyptian desert. It touched down after 19 days and nearly 22 hours, having covered 40,814 kilometres (25,361 miles). Piccard and Jones had achieved the greatest ballooning challenge of all time.

TOOLS OF THE TRADE

Breitling Orbiter 3 combined two types of balloon technology. The tall upper balloon was filled with the gas helium, which is lighter than air. At the base was a cone-shaped hot-air balloon. By burning propane gas, Piccard and Jones could heat the air inside the hot-air balloon to make it rise. As the air inside cooled, the balloon descended. If they needed to descend quickly, Piccard and Jones could actively release hot air from the balloon. Despite improvements in technology, they were still not able to steer the balloon accurately. To succeed, they needed good winds and a large slice of luck!

MELVILL AND BINNIE
SHOT INTO SPACE

Wearing an astronaut-style flying suit, pilot Brian Binnie slipped into the cockpit of an odd-looking plane called *SpaceShipOne*. The date was 4 October 2004. If the test flight Binnie was about to make was successful, his team would win $10 million (£6.6 million). If it failed, the team would get nothing. The pressure was on!

SpaceShipOne was designed to carry three people. On the test flights it carried just the pilot, with sandbags making up the weight of another two passengers.

Then and now

During the history of aviation, cash prizes had regularly tempted fliers to perform amazing feats. In 1909, French aviator Louis Blériot won $1,500 (£1,000) for the first flight across the English Channel. In 1927, American flier Charles Lindbergh won $25,000 (£16,500) for the first solo flight across the Atlantic Ocean. Cash prizes also encouraged aircraft designers, such as Burt Rutan, to come up with pioneering plane designs.

The Ansari X Prize

In 1996, an organization called the X Foundation offered $10 million to any company that could build a plane able to reach space twice in a fortnight. The X Foundation defined space as 100 kilometres (62 miles) above Earth's surface. No fewer than 26 teams all over the world took up the challenge to build a reusable spaceplane, but by autumn 2004 still no one had succeeded. The deadline for the prize was 1 January 2005, so time was fast running out.

In the United States, a company called Mojave Aerospace Ventures (MAV) had teamed up with Burt Rutan, who had designed both *Voyager* (see pages 10–12) and Steve Fossett's *GlobalFlyer* (see page 13). From the start, Rutan knew that to succeed he must overcome two main problems. The first was the safe ground launch of a spaceplane; the second was the plane's re-entry into Earth's atmosphere, which can cause any spacecraft to burn up.

Burt Rutan (right) in front of *SpaceShipOne* with investor Paul Allen (left). Astronaut Mike Melvill (centre) was *SpaceShipOne*'s pilot for its first flight into space.

Rutan figured out a way to solve both problems. He decided to avoid the danger of ground launch by launching from a carrier aircraft. He overcame the second problem, re-entering Earth's atmosphere, by giving the spaceplane a unique shuttlecock design.

First flight

By 2004, Rutan had built the carrier aircraft *White Knight*, and a spaceplane that he believed could reach space and return safely. Pilot Mike Melvill was chosen for the first test flight on 21 June 2004. *White Knight* carried Melvill and *SpaceShipOne* to a height of 15,000 metres (50,000 feet) before releasing the spaceplane. Melvill rocketed to the edge of space and glided back to Earth when his fuel had been used up.

TOOLS OF THE TRADE

Particles in Earth's atmosphere bombard a spacecraft's shell as it re-enters the atmosphere at speed, creating intense heat. Rutan reduced the chances of his craft burning up by finding a way to slow down its flight before re-entry. His design used brake flaps on the wings and a moveable tail, which could be lifted to create drag. It was called the shuttlecock design because the feathers of a badminton shuttlecock create drag in a similar way.

The *White Knight* aircraft carries *SpaceShipOne* over the Mojave desert in California. A combination of factors make air launch much safer for a spacecraft, including the fact that the craft has to carry less fuel and so is lighter. This means that it does not experience as much resistance during takeoff and so heat against its shell.

Going for the record

With time running out, the MAV team decided *SpaceShipOne* was ready to go for the record. To win the prize, the team would need to make two trips into space in as many weeks. Mike Melvill was again chosen for the first flight on 29 September. After release from *White Knight*, *SpaceShipOne* shot upwards faster than a bullet. Melvill had to fight the controls to right the plane as it began rolling, which could have spelled disaster. He controlled the roll and eventually glided down to a safe landing.

From G-force to weightlessness, the pilots of *SpaceShipOne*'s two blasts into space got the ride of their lives. *White Knight* and *SpaceShipOne* were retired from service immediately following the prize-winning second flight.

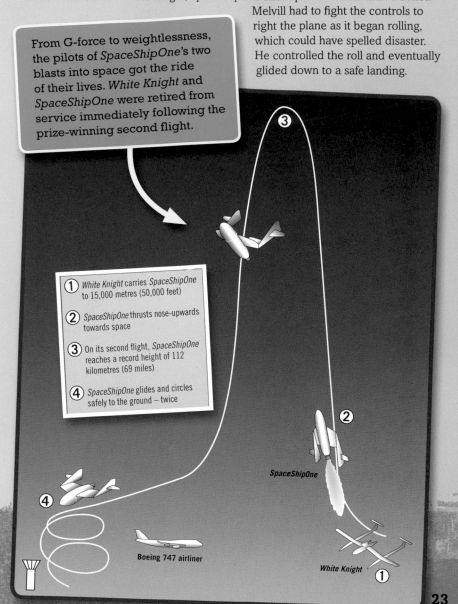

(1) *White Knight* carries *SpaceShipOne* to 15,000 metres (50,000 feet)

(2) *SpaceShipOne* thrusts nose-upwards towards space

(3) On its second flight, *SpaceShipOne* reaches a record height of 112 kilometres (69 miles)

(4) *SpaceShipOne* glides and circles safely to the ground – twice

SpaceShipOne

Boeing 747 airliner

White Knight

Now it was all down to pilot Brian Binnie. On 4 October, Melvill in *White Knight* carried Binnie and *SpaceShipOne* to the test height. Shortly after release, Binnie fired the rocket motor and pointed the nose upwards. The spaceplane zoomed towards space at around 4,280 kilometres per hour (2,660 miles per hour), reaching a record height of 112 kilometres (69 miles), this time without rolling.

For more than 3 minutes, Binnie experienced weightlessness. Then he flipped on the braking system and headed downwards to re-enter Earth's atmosphere. With the plane safely landed, MAV had won the X Prize!

"This is real first-class, top-line rocket science executed to an incredible degree of precision. This flight couldn't have been any smoother."
Paul Allen

Pilot Brian Binnie inside the cockpit of *SpaceShipOne* during the spacecraft's prize-winning second spaceflight.

Space tourism

The success of *SpaceShipOne* marked the start of space tourism. British businessman and Virgin Group boss Richard Branson (see pages 16–17) teamed up with Burt Rutan to form a new company, Virgin Galactic. Their aim is to give paying customers the chance to ride in space. More than 500 people, including many celebrities, have now booked a flight, at a cost of around $200,000 (£132,200) each.

Dennis Tito

In 2001, American businessman Dennis Tito became the first space tourist. He paid an estimated $20 million (£13.2 million) for a return trip on a Russian rocket to the International Space Station (see pages 26–31). For Tito, the trip was worth every cent. Burt Rutan is now working on a design that will allow tourists to visit a space station. One day in the not-too-distant future, there may even be hotels in space.

Dennis Tito (far left) with the Commander and Flight Engineer from his space tourist flight. Of his trip, Tito later said: "I spent 60 years on Earth and I spent 8 days in space. From my viewpoint, it was two separate lives."

TEAM DISCOVERY
OVERCOMING DISASTER

Excitement was running high as Commander Eileen Collins led her crew aboard Space Shuttle *Discovery* on 26 July 2005. Collins was in charge of the first American spaceflight since a disastrous Shuttle mission in 2003 that ended with the loss of all seven of its crew.

Reusable spacecraft

The Space Shuttle programme began in 1981. It was the first major space programme by NASA (the American space agency) since the Apollo Moon programme of the 1960s and 1970s. The Space Shuttle was designed to be the world's first reusable spacecraft. Booster rockets delivered the craft into space, where it performed all sorts of tasks before returning to Earth and landing like a plane.

Mission Commander Eileen Collins (front right) leads the crew of *Discovery* to a transfer van. The van will take them all to a launchpad where they will board the Space Shuttle and prepare for takeoff.

Early disasters

NASA built six Space Shuttles in all. However, two met with disaster. In 1986, Space Shuttle *Challenger* exploded shortly after takeoff, killing all seven of its crew. NASA cancelled all missions while engineers improved the safety of the remaining Space Shuttles. The programme restarted two years later, but in 2003 Space Shuttle *Columbia* burned up while re-entering Earth's atmosphere. Experts discovered that foam leaking from the fuel tank at takeoff had damaged tiles on the underside of the plane that protected it from the intense heat of re-entry.

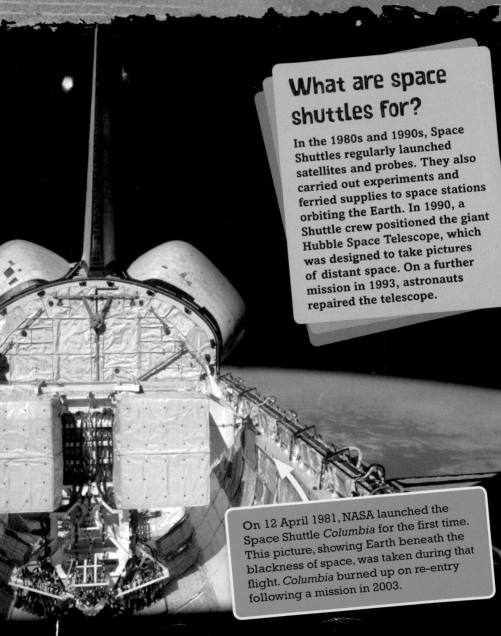

What are space shuttles for?

In the 1980s and 1990s, Space Shuttles regularly launched satellites and probes. They also carried out experiments and ferried supplies to space stations orbiting the Earth. In 1990, a Shuttle crew positioned the giant Hubble Space Telescope, which was designed to take pictures of distant space. On a further mission in 1993, astronauts repaired the telescope.

On 12 April 1981, NASA launched the Space Shuttle *Columbia* for the first time. This picture, showing Earth beneath the blackness of space, was taken during that flight. *Columbia* burned up on re-entry following a mission in 2003.

Extreme forces

Now Collins and her crew prepared for takeoff on the first mission after the *Columbia* disaster. The whole world was watching. As the booster rockets fired, the shaking was so violent that the crew could hardly see the instruments. They experienced the extreme stress known as G-force, which pushed them back in their seats, as the rocket roared upwards.

Each Space Shuttle that NASA built was intended to make 100 flights into space – each time carrying precious cargo, such as items for re-stocking the International Space Station. By the end of the Space Shuttle programme, *Discovery* had undertaken the greatest number of missions – 39 of them, covering more than 238 million kilometres (148 million miles) in total.

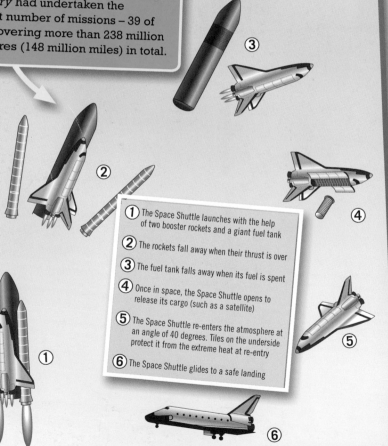

① The Space Shuttle launches with the help of two booster rockets and a giant fuel tank

② The rockets fall away when their thrust is over

③ The fuel tank falls away when its fuel is spent

④ Once in space, the Space Shuttle opens to release its cargo (such as a satellite)

⑤ The Space Shuttle re-enters the atmosphere at an angle of 40 degrees. Tiles on the underside protect it from the extreme heat at re-entry

⑥ The Space Shuttle glides to a safe landing

Commander Eileen Collins

Eileen Collins worked as a test pilot and military instructor in the US Air Force before being selected as an astronaut. After three years of intense training, in 1995 she became the first-ever female Space Shuttle pilot. In 1999, Collins became the first female Space Shuttle commander. Her experience and unflappable calm made her the ideal choice to lead NASA's return to space in 2005.

Safety hitch

Discovery soon reached space and the crew experienced freedom from Earth's gravity. Their mission was to check new safety features on the Space Shuttle and to take essential supplies to the crew on the International Space Station (ISS). However, all was not well. Foam from the fuel tank had again struck the craft during takeoff. If there was any serious damage, *Discovery* would meet the same fate as *Columbia* when it attempted re-entry.

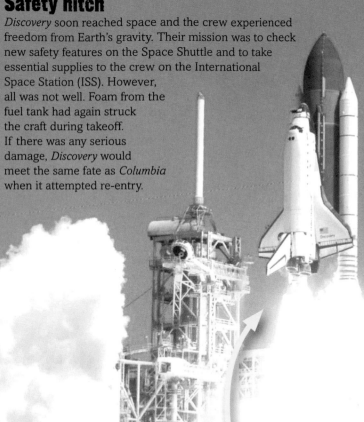

Discovery launches amid a cloud of fiery gases on 26 July 2005. It would take Commander Collins and her team 2 days to reach the International Space Station.

29

On the mission

Discovery headed towards the International Space Station (ISS). Once there, Collins had to fly the Space Shuttle in a 360-degree rotation so that the ISS crew could check for damage. This was the first time this manoeuvre had ever been flown. Luckily, there seemed to be no damage, but re-entry was still a worry.

This picture of the International Space Station was taken from *Discovery* during the 2005 space mission. You can see the blue of the Caspian Sea on Earth below.

After a mission lasting 15 days, *Discovery* headed for home. Despite concerns, the Shuttle survived the intense heat of re-entry, landing safely. It was mission accomplished for Commander Collins.

"[As an astronaut] it is especially important to work well as a team, to get along with all co-workers. You will have bumps on the road along the way. Take every disappointment in your career as an opportunity for something new and better in the future."
Eileen Collins

30

What next for space travel?

The Space Shuttle programme ended in 2011. Since then, NASA has continued its programme of unmanned exploration. It is now developing a new Space Launch System and the *Orion* spacecraft, with the aims of returning to the Moon and visiting Mars. Meanwhile, in 2013, Dennis Tito (see page 25) announced plans for a privately funded mission to send a man and woman to Mars, due to launch in 2018. The return trip will take 501 days.

Shannon Lucid

Eileen Collins logged a total of 36 days in space on her four missions. However, fellow American astronaut Shannon Lucid, who spent 188 days aboard Space Station *Mir* in 1996, easily beat her total. Speaking of the difficulties of becoming a woman astronaut, Lucid said: "Basically, all my life I'd been told you can't do that because you're female. So I guess I just didn't pay any attention."

Shannon Lucid's stay on *Mir* was longer than planned because of problems with the Space Shuttle *Atlantis* that would eventually bring her back to Earth. In this picture, she is using a treadmill aboard *Mir* to keep fit.

YVES ROSSY
ROCKET-POWERED JETMAN

Is it a bird? Is it a plane? Is it Superman? No, it's Swiss aviator and inventor Yves Rossy! Since 2006, Rossy has been taking to the air with his own personal jetpack. He claims to be the world's one and only "Jetman".

Early flying feats

Born in 1959, Rossy flew fighter jets for the Swiss Air Force for 17 years. Then he switched to flying commercial planes. In the 1990s, Rossy established a string of flying records. In 1994, he launched from a plane and "skysurfed" on a board resembling a snowboard, before parachuting to the ground. In 1996, he held on between the wings of two biplanes in flight, earning himself an entry in the *Guinness World Records* book. In 2002, he soared above Lake Geneva, Switzerland, on an inflatable wing, having launched from an aircraft.

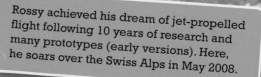

Rossy achieved his dream of jet-propelled flight following 10 years of research and many prototypes (early versions). Here, he soars over the Swiss Alps in May 2008.

The jetpack

Rossy was making headlines, but his dream was to fly under his own jet-propulsion (driving force). In the 1990s, he began working on a design for a jetpack with a rigid wing, powered by jet engines. In 2006, he tested the jetpack in a flight that lasted 5 minutes and 40 seconds. Two years later, he made his first official flight, zooming through the air at 200 kilometres per hour (125 miles per hour).

The jetpack's rigid wings are made of carbon fibre and span 2 metres (6 feet 6 inches). The four jet engines on the underside of the wings are adapted from model aircraft engines. The whole pack weighs a hefty 55 kilograms (121 pounds).

TOOLS OF THE TRADE

The jetpack has no built-in steering. Rossy uses his own body to steer the wing. He arches his back to climb, and pushes his shoulders forwards to dive. He can even loop the loop!

The Channel and beyond

Since those first flights, Rossy has set many records. In 2008, he crossed the English Channel from Calais, France, to Dover, England. He made the 35-kilometre (22-mile) crossing in just 13 minutes. The following year, he attempted another first – to fly between two continents, Africa and Europe. His plan had been to cross the Strait of Gibraltar from Morocco to Spain, but, unfortunately, strong winds and dense clouds forced him to ditch into the Mediterranean. A helicopter picked him up unhurt.

Yves Rossy leapt from a helicopter to soar over the Grand Canyon, Arizona, USA, in May 2011.

TOOLS OF THE TRADE

A typical Jetman flightplan involves catching a ride to high altitude on a plane, helicopter, or hot-air balloon. Rossy then fires his jetpack engines and leaps from the launch craft to fly under his own propulsion. When his fuel is used up, he parachutes to the ground.

In 2010, at a height of 2,400 metres (7,900 feet), Rossy launched a new-look jetpack from a hot-air balloon flown by Brian Jones (see pages 14–19). The following year, he zoomed along the majestic Grand Canyon in Arizona, United States, one of the world's deepest gorges. In 2012, he made several flights alongside aircraft, giving amazed passengers a close-up view of jet-propulsion. No one knows exactly what he will do next, but whatever it is, it is bound to be amazing!

"I love to fly, and to fly like this is freedom. The emotions are so strong you become addicted."
Yves "Jetman" Rossy

Yves Rossy flying in tandem with a World-War-II Spitfire plane.

FELIX BAUMGARTNER
LEAP INTO SPACE

Austrian skydiver Felix Baumgartner opened the door of the balloon capsule and climbed onto the step. At an altitude of 39 kilometres (24 miles), he could see Earth curving below him. A pressurized suit protected him from intense cold and lack of oxygen. It was 14 October 2012, and Baumgartner was about to attempt the world's highest-ever parachute jump.

Early life

Born in 1969, Felix Baumgartner dreamed of flying and skydiving from an early age. He made his first parachute jump at 16. Joining the Austrian military as a paratrooper, he learned to parachute down onto a small target. After working as a motorcycle mechanic, he became a professional skydiver and BASE jumper.

Baumgartner gets ready to leap from the capsule in 2012. "Sometimes you have to be up really high to see how small you are," he later said.

Baumgartner prepares to BASE jump from the Christ the Redeemer statue, Rio de Janeiro, Brazil, in 1999.

Daring leaps

In the 1990s and 2000s, Baumgartner became famous for a series of daring parachute jumps. In 1999, he BASE jumped from the Petronas Towers, Kuala Lumpur, Malaysia. In 2003, he jumped from a plane to freefall across the English Channel, using a wing to steer himself through the sky. In 2007, he BASE jumped from Taipei 101 in Taiwan, then the world's tallest building.

TOOLS OF THE TRADE

BASE jumping is the practice of leaping and parachuting down from a fixed point, such as a building. The term BASE comes from the first letters of the four main types of fixed points that jumpers use: buildings, antennae (masts) span (bridges), and earth (cliffs). The jumper has only seconds in freefall before the parachute opens.

Stratosphere jump

In 2010, Baumgartner announced plans to attempt the world's highest skydive, from the stratosphere. Baumgartner would travel to the upper stratosphere in a pressurized capsule under a helium balloon. He hoped to break the current skydiving record, which had been set by American skydiver Joe Kittinger back in 1960. At 84 years old, Kittinger had generously agreed to act as Baumgartner's ground-based advisor – one of a team of experts who supported the jump.

Joe Kittinger in 1960 shortly before his historic jump from the stratosphere. His freefall lasted for 4 minutes and 36 seconds.

Preparing for the big one

Baumgartner made several test jumps to prepare for his "Red Bull Stratos" leap. In July 2012, he jumped from an altitude of 29.6 kilometres (almost 18½ miles). He spent about 3 minutes and 50 seconds in freefall before opening his parachute. He also had to spend time wearing the specially made pressurized suit. At first, the suit made him feel claustrophobic, but he conquered his fear.

> "There's no way you can visualize the speed. There's nothing you can see to judge how fast you're going. You know you are going very fast, but you don't feel it."
> **Joe Kittinger**

Joe Kittinger

Colonel Joseph Kittinger is a former pilot in the US Air Force. In August 1960, he rode the balloon *Excelsior III* to the record height of 31 kilometres (19 miles), and then jumped. In doing so, he helped open the door to the space age and set four important records. These were: highest balloon ascent, highest parachute jump, longest freefall time, and fastest-ever freefall – his top speed was 988 kilometres per hour (614 miles per hour). Kittinger is a record-breaking balloonist, too. He made the first solo crossing of the Atlantic Ocean in a balloon.

Felix Baumgartner and Joe Kittinger shake hands at a press conference following Baumgartner's historic jump.

Jumper away!

At 9.28 a.m. on 14 October 2012, Baumgartner's helium balloon was launched from Roswell International Air Center, New Mexico, United States. Two-and-a-half hours later, secured inside a capsule attached to the balloon, Baumgartner reached a height of 39 kilometres (24 miles) – the highest a manned balloon had ever flown. He de-pressurized the capsule, opened the door, stepped out, and leapt into thin air. "Jumper away!" said Mission Control on the audio.

In a spin

Seconds into his freefall, however, it appeared that Baumgartner might be in serious trouble. He seemed to go into a fast spin. Everyone on the ground held their breath in fear, but eventually Baumgartner managed to control his fall. Plummeting through the air, he reached a record speed of 1,357 kilometres per hour (843 miles per hour). At Mach 1.25, Baumgartner was falling faster than the speed of sound!

> "The only thing standing between you and your goal is the story you keep telling yourself as to why you can't achieve it."
> **Felix Baumgartner**

This photograph was taken from the capsule as Baumgartner leapt off his platform and hurtled towards Earth. Eight million internet users simultaneously watched the jump.

After 4 minutes and 20 seconds of freefall, Baumgartner opened his parachute. Five minutes later, he landed on his feet and raised his arms in victory. The Austrian had smashed three of Joe Kittinger's records – the American still held the record for the longest freefall time – and, importantly, his mission had gathered data that will help to improve the safety of space exploration.

What next?

By an amazing coincidence, Baumgartner's jump on 14 October occurred exactly 65 years to the day after Chuck Yeager (see pages 4–5) broke the sound barrier in the Bell X-1 in 1947. Sixty-five years before, no one even dreamed that it would be possible for a person to travel at supersonic speed without a plane. No one knows what the next 65 years of aviation will bring, but one thing is certain: audacious aviators will accomplish feats that we can hardly even imagine today.

Safely landed back on Earth, Baumgartner celebrates his record-breaking leap. The capsule in which he had ascended landed 16 kilometres (10 miles) further east.

TiMELINE

1783 Pilâtre de Rozier and the Marquis d'Arlandes (France) make the first manned hot-air balloon flight, in a balloon designed and built by the Montgolfier brothers

1909 Louis Blériot (France) is the first person to fly across the English Channel

1927 Charles Lindbergh (USA) makes the first solo flight across the Atlantic Ocean

1933 Pilot Wiley Post (USA) flies solo around the world

1947 Pilot Chuck Yeager (USA) is the first to fly at supersonic speed in the Bell X-1 plane

1960 Aviator Joe Kittinger (USA) sets the world record for the highest-ever manned balloon flight and parachute jump

1967 The US rocketplane X-15 flies at Mach 6.7

1976 Supersonic jetliner *Concorde* enters service, flying passengers between London, England, and New York, USA

1977 Aviator and cyclist Bryan Allen (USA) achieves the first-ever human-powered flight in the *Gossamer Condor*

1979 Bryan Allen makes the first human-powered flight across the English Channel in the *Gossamer Albatross*

1981 US space agency NASA launches the Space Shuttle programme

1986 Dick Rutan and Jeana Yeager (USA) complete the first non-stop flight around the world without refuelling

1995 Eileen Collins (USA) becomes the first female Space Shuttle pilot

1999 Bertrand Piccard (Switzerland) and Brian Jones (UK) achieve the first round-the-world balloon flight in *Breitling Orbiter 3*

2001 Businessman Dennis Tito (USA) becomes the first space tourist

2003 Supersonic jetliner *Concorde* is retired from service

2004 *SpaceShipOne* becomes the first private spacecraft to reach space twice in a fortnight, and wins the Ansari X Prize

2005 Aviator Steve Fossett (USA) achieves the first solo round-the-world flight without refuelling

2008 Yves "Jetman" Rossy (Switzerland) makes his first official flight

2012 Skydiver Felix Baumgartner (Austria) sets a new record for the highest-ever manned balloon flight and parachute jump by leaping from 39 kilometres (24 miles) above Earth

Are you mad about planes and flying? Do you enjoy finding out how machines work?

a Yes, I find aircraft fascinating. I love taking machines apart to see how they work.

b I like the idea of flying, but I'm not really mechanically minded.

c I'm not that bothered about planes, and if I take something apart, I can never put it back together again.

Are you good at fast and furious sports such as skiing, snowboarding, skateboarding, or biking, which require good balance and quick reactions?

a The faster the better! I love the rush and rarely take a spill.

b I do OK at sports that require balance and quick reactions, but I'm not the best.

c Sport isn't really my thing, or at any rate I'd rather watch than take part.

What's your co-ordination like when you play computer games and simulations?

a Pretty good. I usually win or get the highest score.

b I do OK, but I'm not usually the best.

c I tend to crash or come in last when I play computer games.

Have you got a head for heights?

a Heights don't bother me at all.

b I can cope, but sheer drops make me a bit uneasy.

c I'm scared stiff of heights.

ANSWERS:

Mostly a: Looks like you've got what it takes to be a daring aviator – quick responses, good co-ordination, and a love of speed and flying machines.

Mostly b: You may have what it takes to be an audacious aviator, but you need to work on your reactions and co-ordination.

Mostly c: Aviation doesn't seem to be your thing at the moment, but perhaps you have yet to be bitten by the flying bug!

GLOSSARY

accelerate to go faster

aeronautics design and construction of aircraft

altitude height above sea level

BASE jumping jumping and parachuting from a fixed point, such as a building or cliff

biplane plane with two wings, one above the other

capsule sealed cabin of a plane, balloon, or spacecraft

circumnavigate to travel completely around the world

claustrophobia fear of small spaces

cockpit part of a plane where the pilot sits with the controls

drag force that holds back an aircraft as it moves forwards through the air

ejector seat seat in a plane that blasts the pilot out of the plane in an emergency, so that he or she can land using a parachute

freefall falling without a parachute

fuselage main body of an aeroplane

G-force force felt on the body as a result of gravity or acceleration

gondola cabin of an airship or balloon

helium gas that is lighter than air

International Space Station (ISS) space station that orbits Earth and is used by astronauts from many different nations

jet engine engine that produces thrust by forcing hot gases out of a nozzle at the back

jet stream powerful winds that blow at high altitude

lift upwards force that helps aeroplanes – and birds – to fly

Mach 1 speed of sound; in dry, warm air, this is about 1,236 kilometres per hour (768 miles per hour), while Mach 2 is twice the speed of sound

malfunction when something does not work properly

paratrooper soldier trained to use a parachute

pressurized cockpit, cabin, or balloon gondola that is supplied with air at a comfortable pressure

propane gas that can be burned as fuel

propulsion driving force that produces movement

prototype early version or model

rocket motor engine that works like a jet engine

roll when a plane tilts so that one wing rises and the other falls

shuttlecock cone-shaped object, traditionally made with feathers, batted between players in the game of badminton

sonic boom loud sound that is heard when a plane goes supersonic

sound barrier name given to the imaginary point or obstacle that marks the speed of sound

stratosphere layer in Earth's atmosphere, 10 to 50 kilometres (30,000 to 160,000 feet) above Earth's surface

supersonic faster than the speed of sound

thrust force that drives an aircraft or rocket

FIND OUT MORE

Books

Aircraft (How Machines Work), Ian Graham (Franklin Watts, 2008)

Aircraft (Sci-Hi), Andrew Solway (Raintree, 2011)

Flight (Insiders), Von Hardesty (Templar Publishing, 2008)

The World of Flight, Ian Graham (Kingfisher, 2006)

Websites

www.airandspace.si.edu
Uncover fascinating information about the history of flight and space exploration.

www.felixbaumgartner.com
Felix Baumgartner's personal website gives insight into his leap into space, and his other feats of adventure.

www.jetman.com
See some amazing pictures of Yves "Jetman" Rossy and learn more about his rocket-powered wings.

www.museumofflight.org/education
The website of the United States' Museum of Flight charts the history of aviation.

www.nasa.gov
The United States' space agency website has news, images, and interactive features about all aspects of space and the history of flight.

www.nasa.gov/centers/dryden/home/index

The Dryden Flight Research Center is a division of NASA. This website gives more images, videos, and interactive features from the space agency.

www.scaled.com

Scaled Composites is the company founded by aviation pioneer Burt Rutan (see page 21) and the website has loads of information about and images of *GlobalFlyer*, *White Knight*, and *SpaceShipOne*.

Further research

Do some digging on the Montgolfier brothers. What can you find out about their early lives? What do you think inspired them to build a hot-air balloon? What were their first balloons made from?

Dick Rutan and Jeana Yeager were the first to circumnavigate the globe without refuelling, but who made the first-ever flight in an aircraft? Do some research into the very beginnings of aviation.

Jacqueline Cochran is thought to have set more than 200 world records. Find out what some of them are and how many of them, if any, still stand. What can you find out about other great women aviators?

Draw a family tree for the Piccard family. Label it with the family's inventions, adventures, and records.

INDEX